CALLED TO WAR

HOW LIFE'S BATTLES TRANSFORM US FOR GOD'S PURPOSES

DAWN AMSDEN STARK

Called to War: How Life's Battles Transform Us for God's Purposes/Dawn Amsden Stark

Copyright @2021 by Dawn Marie Stark

Published in the United States of America

Library of Congress Control Number: 2021916785

All Scripture quotations are taken from the Holy Bible, New International Version®, NIV®. Copyright © 1973, 1978, 1984, 2011 by Biblica, Inc.™ Used by permission of Zondervan. All rights reserved worldwide. www.zondervan.com. The "NIV" and "New International Version" are trademarks registered in the United States Patent and Trademark Office by Biblica, Inc.™

Editing by Leanne Wickham of Red Pencil
Proofreading Typesetting by Sally Hanan of Inksnatcher.com

Cover design by Jessica Salas of Alas Creative Design
Original cover and chapter art by Isabelle Stark

Study Guide ISBN: 978-1-7374916-2-0

Book ISBNs: 978-1-7374916-0-6 (paperback) | ISBN 978-1-7374916-1-3 (hardback) | ISBN 978-1-7374916-2-0 (e-book)

TABLE OF CONTENTS

Letter from Dawn i
1. Conscription Notice 1
2. Reporting Orders 4
3. Boot Camp 7
4. Life as a Soldier 10
5. Commander-in-Chief 13
6. Tactics and Strategies 16
7. Death Days and Memorial Stones 20
8. Weapons of War 23
9. A Spy Named Fear 26
10. Terms of Surrender 29
11. A Peace Treaty 32
12. The Battle for Your Promises 34
13. Rest, Recuperation, and Reassignment 37
14. The Final Battle 40
15. A New War 43
16. Overseas Duty Station 46
17. Returning Home 49
18. Special Forces 52
19. –20. New Eyes, New Heart, and a New Walk.... 55
About the Author 59

LETTER FROM DAWN

Called to War tells the story of my personal transformation that occurred over the course of a twenty-three-year infertility and adoption journey. This book helps us understand how life's battles transform us for God's purposes. Framed metaphorically in militaristic language, *Called to War* tells a story of surrender while at the same time imparts important lessons and rewards of a life lived in sacrifice for others.

The concept of transformation is not unique to me. It also applies to you. Scripture is filled with stories of transformation and encouragement for this process. I believe it's a journey we are all called to live. I call this process repurposing—to change [something] so that it can be used for a different purpose.

I've invited you into my story. Now I'm calling you to some of the hard heart work needed in your own journey of transformation through the questions contained in this study guide. I hope that by sharing my story, you too will be able to identify processes of transformation in your own life.

Ultimately, my prayer is that you will find the courage to surrender to the Sovereign. Our compassionate and loving Commander-in-Chief desires to give you new eyes, a new heart, and a new walk so that you might wholeheartedly embrace His plans for your life.

1

Conscription Notice

This opening chapter sets up a few threads of my backstory to help you understand the foundations of my life and faith experience. I was only a child, both naturally and spiritually, which meant that I sought after the temporal and imminent aspects of life. Even at a young age, American individualism and notions of freedom shaped how I interacted with my faith. Thankfully, God's perspective oversaw my entire story and he continued to prepare me for the future while I only had eyes to see the present.

Your story will not be like mine, as we all have unique journeys and callings. Here are a few questions to help you identify the faith foundations in your life as we engage on this called to war journey together:

1. What is your salvation story?

2. What was your early church experience?

3. Did you ever feel called to a specific aspect of ministry or service?

4. Do you recall a book, sermon, testimony, or personal experience that was significant in shifting the direction of your life?

5. Can you identify a place in your life where the goals you set for yourself might have been different from what God wanted for your life?

6. Can you recall a time when a fantasy met reality causing your perspective to shift?

7. What does a missionary look like to you?

8. What impacted you most about this chapter?

Verses to Contemplate

John 4:35–37: Don't you have a saying, 'It's still four months until harvest'? I tell you, open your eyes and look at the fields! They are ripe for harvest. Even now the one who reaps draws a wage and harvests a crop for eternal life, so that the sower and the reaper may be glad together. Thus the saying 'one sows and another reaps' is true.

Psalm 37:23–25: The LORD makes firm the steps of the one who delights in him; though he may stumble, he will not fall, for the LORD upholds him with his hand. I was young and now I am old, yet I have never seen the righteous forsaken or their children begging bread.

Chapter 1

2

Reporting Orders

Growing up always involves the collapse of the naiveté of childhood; this is one of the great transitions we all experience as people. Our ideals and expectations of what life should look like is often forged by the people who raise us, as well as the norms of the culture in which we live. My white, American, Christian, middle-class upbringing might be radically different than yours, but we share the commonality of passing from children to adulthood together. We also share dreams, disappointments, milestones, and the joys of the human experience.

As a person of faith, there is a point where you begin to see the intervention of a heavenly story or destiny being written in your life. Here are a few questions to help you reflect back on your story and identify where you began to journey with God:

1. When you were growing up, what did adult life look like to you?

2. Do you recall the first place in your life where you had to surrender your dreams or desires to God?

3. Where can you look back now in your journey and see a place or time God issued your "conscription notice?"

4. Can you identify any metaphorical "reporting orders" in your story?

5. What was your attitude when you received "reporting orders" you did not request?

6. Do you remember any particular "mercies in the process" during this time in your life?

7. What impacted you most about this chapter?

Verses to Contemplate

Matthew 10:39: Whoever finds their life will lose it, and whoever loses their life for my sake will find it.

Psalm 30:4–5: Sing the praises of the Lord, you his faithful people, praise his holy name. For his anger lasts only a moment, but his favor lasts a lifetime; weeping may stay for the night, but rejoicing comes in the morning.

Called to War Study Guide

3

Boot Camp

As you read my story, you learned about several wars I've been called to fight throughout my life. Without a doubt, my infertility war was the longest and most painful. Eventually, I was able to see that my battles with infertility were equally my most transformational. I was the worst recruit in the beginning. My boot camp experience was ugly and painful because I was naïve and lived in denial for too long.

As we enter this part of the book, I ask you to please remember that the material is framed metaphorically in militaristic language in order to examine and understand the battles we all face in life. I invite you now to apply this same language to your transformation story, whether this event is one you've endured in the past or one you are currently fighting.

Here are a few questions to help you process your book camp experience:

1. Is there a particular traumatic event in your life that substantially impacted your future?

2. Can you name your boot camp?

3. What is something significant you have been denied?

4. How do you respond to denial?

5. What does living out of control mean and look like for you?

6. What can you learn from Hannah's story in 1 Samuel 1?

7. What impacted you most about this chapter?

Verses to Contemplate

1 Samuel 1:10–11: In her deep anguish Hannah prayed to the Lord, weeping bitterly. And she made a vow, saying, "Lord Almighty, if you will only look on your servant's misery and remember me, and not forget your servant but give her a son, then I will give him to the Lord for all the days of his life, and no razor will ever be used on his head."

Chapter 3

4

Life as a Soldier

One of the challenges in our transformation process is that we cannot see the greater narrative of our life in advance since clarity only fully comes in hindsight. This requires us to have trust in our Commander, even when we cannot see clearly or understand fully the context of what's occurring in our story. Transformation requires faith, which is God's gift to us if we will onlytrust him to masterfully weave together our story.

The process of transformation is constant throughout our lives, both physically and spiritually. The majority of us are born with physical eyes butoften the development of spiritual eyes only occurs after we adapt the posture of submission and surrender to God.

Here are a few questions to think through about your own transformation process:

1. Can you identify any specialized training after your boot camp experience that was important in advancing your story?

2. Considering the puzzle analogy, what pieces do you have in your hand that don't appear to fit in your picture? What pieces do you not like?

Chapter 4

3. Can you relate to a messy situation getting messier? What does this look like in your life?

4. Can you identify any mercies in your process at this stage of your transformation?

5. How can delay make you stronger?

6. How is delayed different than denied?

7. What impacted you most about this chapter?

VERSES TO CONTEMPLATE

Psalm 94:18–19: When I said, "My foot is slipping," your unfailing love, Lord, supported me. When anxiety was great within me, your consolation brought me joy.

Hebrews 11:6: And without faith it is impossible to please God, because anyone who comes to him must believe that he exists and that he rewards those who earnestly seek him.

Called to War Study Guide

5

Commander-in-Chief

Trust is a major theme in this chapter. Our ability to trust others (horizontal trust) and God (vertical trust) is critically important to our ability to lead authentic, whole, and meaningful lives. However, it's nearly impossible to surrender to God if we do not understand who He is and his promises over us. Scripture tells us God is the maker of heaven and earth, man's breath of life, and the author of each of our stories. Learning more about God's character and nature is a big key in learning how we can trust our Heavenly Father so that we can willingly give him control over our lives.

Yet many of us, even though we may be born again, struggle intrinsically to trust God's sovereignty in our lives. To varying degrees, we all resist surrendering control, even when our lives are messy and broken. This is true even when we know God's ways are perfect. Here are a few questions to guide you through your current relationship with your Commander-in-Chief:

1. How are trust and obedience connected? What does this mean in your life?

2. Trust is risky. What scares you the most about trusting others (horizontal trust)? Trusting God (vertical trust)?

3. What is a situation in your life where your horizontal trust has been abused? How could this situation be affecting your vertical trust?

4. How are faith and trust tied together?

5. In this chapter we read author W. Pink's description of the sovereignty of God written in 1918. How did you feel about his description?

6. Considering the many names of God in scripture, which one is the most significant to you?

7. Which part of Job's story do you struggle to understand? How does God's reply to Job (chapters 38-41) help you resolve this tension?

8. What impacted you the most in this chapter?

VERSES TO CONTEMPLATE

Mark 12:30–31: Love the Lord your God with all your heart and with all your soul and with all your mind and with all your strength.' The second is this: 'Love your neighbor as yourself.' There is no commandment greater than these.

Chapter 5

1 Chronicles 29:11–12: Yours, LORD, is the greatness and the power and the glory and the majesty and the splendor, for everything in heaven and earth is yours. Yours, LORD, is the kingdom; you are exalted as head over all. Wealth and honor come from you; you are the ruler of all things. In your hands are strength and power to exalt and give strength to all.

6

Tactics and Strategies

War is a condition of life, both naturally and spiritually. While these realities of course are very different, similar patterns apply to both. We can find theorieson waging war dating back to the writings of Sun Tzu in the sixth century BC. There is also ample support in Scripture for fighting spiritual wars. In fact, the Bible is filled with war and battle imagery. In this chapter we learned that developing strategies and implementing tactics are critical tools in fighting and winning wars. We also now understand that after boot camp and specialized training conclude, soldiers are deemed battle ready.

In my transformation story, I was called to fight a war named infertility. I don't know what war you are called to fight. Regardless of your personal situation: divorce, handicap, death of a loved one, abuse, depression, miscarriage, terminal illness, or job loss I promise you that God is preparing you for this battle. Better yet, he is right beside you as wage war.

Here are a few questions to help you apply what you've learned in this chapter:

1. Can you name your war?

2. How do you feel about your war?

Chapter 6

3. Considering Sun Tzu's five constant factors, what elements in your war are under your control? What elements are not?

4. Using 'Operation Thanksgiving Dinner' as an example, can you identify the strategies and tactics that may be applicable in your war?

5. As God is constantly present in your situation, where can you see his fingerprints in the form of a pivotal circumstance?

6. A providential relationship?

7. Have you faced any moral or ethical dilemmas in your war? If so, how did you navigate those unique challenges?

8. What particular part of your war has been the most painful: emotionally or physically to endure?

9. What impacted you the most in this chapter?

VERSES TO CONTEMPLATE

Mark 12:30–31: Love the Lord your God with all your heart and with all your soul and with all your mind and with all your strength.' The second is this: 'Love your neighbor as yourself.' There is no commandment greater than these.

Chronicles 29:11–12: Yours, LORD, is the greatness and the power and the glory and the majesty and the splendor, for everything in heaven and earth is yours. Yours, LORD, is the kingdom; you are exalted as head over all. Wealth and honor come from you; you are the ruler of all things. In your hands are strength and power to exalt and give strength to all.

Ephesians 6:12–13: For our struggle is not against flesh and blood, but against the rulers, against the authorities, against the powers of this dark world and against the spiritual forces of evil in the heavenly realms. Therefore put on the full armor of God, so that when the day of evil comes, you may be able to stand your ground, and after you have done everything, to stand.

Chapter 6

7

Death Days and Memorial Stones

Just as war is a condition of life, so is death. Death comes to us all, in many ways and forms. We all are forced to come to terms with tragic finality and devastating endings. Even in those times when we can see death coming, the aftermath of the ending fills us with pain, consumes us with emptiness, and alters our futures in heartbreaking ways. When Heaven says no to our legitimate desires it can be crushing, especially if we are doing exactly the thing we are supposed to be doing when the defeat comes.

When death days arrive in our lives we have to know how to lament and how to build memorial stones. Having never lost a significant person in my life, I did not know how to properly grieve during infertility, especially when facing an intangible loss. I am not sure what type of death day you are facing, but I promise that God is present in your loss. He will teach you how to build memorial stones that will help guide you out of grief.

Here are a few questions to help you process the difficult material we have examined in this chapter:

Chapter 7

1. Have you ever personally faced a death day? If so, do you remember how you made it through the very first day of that loss?

2. Did you feel abandoned by God in your death day?

3. Can you put words to your loss?

4. Have you ever done anything impulsive in the shadow of a loss? If so, how do you view that action now?

5. Do you have hope that you can recover or move forward in life after facing a tragic loss?

6. In your grieving process, what unhealthy ways have you tried to anesthetize your pain?

7. Why are memorial stones important?

8. What impacted you the most in this chapter?

VERSES TO CONTEMPLATE

Psalm 23:1–4: The Lord is my shepherd, I lack nothing. He makes me lie down in green pastures, he leads me beside quiet waters, he refreshes my soul. He guides me along the right paths for his name's sake. Even thoughI walk through the darkest valley, I will fear no evil, for you are with me; your rod and your staff, they comfort me.

> Joshua 4:6–7: In the future, when your children ask you, 'What do these stones mean?' tell them that the flow of the Jordan was cut off before the ark of the covenant of the Lord. When it crossed the Jordan, the waters of the Jordan were cut off. These stones are to be a memorial to the people of Israel forever.

8

Weapons of War

In my infertility war, the natural weapons I held in my hand were money, medication, and technology. When my weapons did not work, I ran away from life and entered a prolonged depression. You see, my weapons and my coping tools were limited. Meanwhile, my Commander-in-Chief desired to give me new spiritual weapons such as worship that would never fail me.

God used pain to gain my attention so that he could teach me a new way to wage war, a holy way. Through worship, I found a way to heal from existing battle wounds and strength for the battles that remained ahead. But most importantly, worship shifted my perspective about the situation. That's the funny thing about letting Heaven do its good and holy work inside our lives. When we "let go and let God," he begins to make all things new.

Here are a few questions to help you think through your weapons of war and to consider the purpose of your pain:

1. Can you identify the natural weapons you use to fight your battles? What are your spiritual weapons?

2. Do you suffer from physical or emotional pain? How do you describe your pain?

3. What does a weapon misfire look like in your situation?

4. Do you see where this might be more harmful than helpful?

5. Worship is both an attitude and an action. How do you worship?

6. Have you ever found a point of surrender or serenity through worship? What does this look like for you?

7. What is a perspective shift you've gained about your story by reading through the examples so far in *Called to War*?

8. What impacted you the most in this chapter?

VERSES TO CONTEMPLATE

Romans 12:1–2: Therefore, I urge you, brothers and sisters, in view of God'smercy, to offer your bodies as a living sacrifice, holy and pleasing to God— this is your true and proper worship. Do not conform to the pattern of this world, but be transformed by the renewing of your mind. Then you will be able to test and approve what God's will is—his good, and perfect will.

Chapter 8

9

A Spy Named Fear

Fear is an insidious spy who quietly and tirelessly plots against us in order to ruin our resolve and weaken our courage. Fear is that constant voice in our ear that tells us to be afraid, to run away, and to give up on whatever war we are fighting. Fear can destroy us from the inside out, without us even knowing what this cloaked enemy is doing silently behind the scenes of our cognitive awareness.

But we do not have to be held captive by fear's powers. When Jesus overcame death, hell, and the grave, he also overcame fear. Jesus put fear under his feet, and so can we through the power available to us in our salvation. In Ephesians 6:17, Paul instructs us to put on the helmet of salvation. Helmets cover our ears, which is where fear whispers its lies. When we are covered by the salvation Jesus freely gives us, we are protected from fear.

Here are a few questions to think through as you identify where fear has a grip on your life:

1. What lie has fear told you over and over again?

2. How can you reframe this lie based on what the Bible promises about your situation?

Chapter 9

3. Can you see ways fear has negatively affected your life?

4. What is the negative self-talk in your head? Can you see where this might be fear's influence?

5. What scripture can you memorize to help you overcome fear's lies?

6. Apart from memorizing scripture, what other change can you make to push back fear's influence over your situation?

7. Where is there hope in your situation?

8. What impacted you the most in this chapter?

Verses to Contemplate

1 Timothy 1:7: For the Spirit God gave us does not make us timid, but gives us power, love and self-discipline.

Proverbs 3:25–26: Have no fear of sudden disaster or of the ruin that overtakes the wicked, for the Lord will be at your side and will keep your foot from being snared.

Called to War Study Guide

10

Terms of Surrender

As I wrote in chapter ten, "In a state of war, failure ultimately leads to surrender." For me, surrender came eight years into my infertility war on the heels of our third failed in-vitro procedure. The story of my life was being written in such a way that it was clear God wanted another direction than the one I dreamed of, for a season at least. After years of battling, I was beginning to understand and surrender to transformation. I finally hit a point where I was able to pick up the metaphorical white flag of surrender and fall on bended knee, not in grief but rather in worship.

There is a point when we all must lay our weapons down, give up our fight, and make peace with our Lord. Actually, I believe the Christian life to be a constant state of surrendering because our Commander is constantly leading us to be transformed.

I don't know where you are currently in your process or if you've been able to accept terms of surrender in your war, but here are a few questions to reflect on regarding the ideas in this chapter:

1. Does the topic of surrender make you angry, sad, hopeless, depressed, or another negative emotion? If so, why might that be?

Called to War Study Guide

2. Can you recognize a place you have been at war with God?

3. Have you surrendered to God's plan for your life, even if it's a difficult path to endure?

4. What does a surrendered life look like in your current situation?

5. Have you personally experienced the upside-down Kingdom of God?

6. Can you ever imagine that your circumstance is actually an ally in your life struggle? How might this look in your life?

7. How can you wholly embrace and authentically enjoy the life you have, not the life you want?

8. What impacted you the most in this chapter?

VERSES TO CONTEMPLATE

Matthew 5:3–12: Jesus said:

"Blessed are the poor in spirit, for theirs is the kingdom of heaven.

Blessed are those who mourn, for they will be comforted.

Blessed are the meek, for they will inherit the earth.

Blessed are those who hunger and thirst for righteousness, for they will be filled.

Blessed are the merciful, for they will be shown mercy.

Blessed are the pure in heart, for they will see God.

Chapter 10

Blessed are the peacemakers, for they will be called children of God.

Blessed are those who are persecuted because of righteousness, for theirs is the kingdom of heaven.

Blessed are you when people insult you, persecute you and falsely say all kinds of evil against you because of me.

Rejoice and be glad, because great is your reward in heaven, for in the same way they persecuted the prophets who were before you."

11

A Peace Treaty

In my book, chapter eleven is a letter written to my unborn child the night before the results of my fourth in-vitro procedure.

I invite you now to take this space to write out a letter to your unfulfilled promise or maybe to write the terms of your peace treaty with the Lord.

Chapter 11

12

The Battle for Your Promises

This part of my story was challenging because I naively believed that warfare was behind me after I was finally pregnant. After conceiving, I assumed that life would resume a normal trajectory towards motherhood and that I would be just like every other pregnant woman. As you learned in this chapter however, that simply was not the case. My identity had changed so much during my ten years with infertility that I had been fundamentally altered and defined by my war. Furthermore, the battle for our firstborn also put my physical life on the line, and that of my miracle baby as well.

You may find your war will come to an end after your peace treaty is drafted. Or, as in my story, your battles may continue even after you've wholly surrendered to the Lord. This is because even though your heart is changed, the battles for your promises might not have ended.

Here are a few questions to help you process through what a post-peace treaty might look like in your unique transformation journey with God:

Chapter 12

1. If the miracle or answered prayer did not occur in your life, what does moving forward after surrendering to God look like to you today?

2. If the miracle or answered prayer occurred in your life, how did you emotionally process that situation?

3. How can you identify with Hannah's prayer in 1 Samuel 2?

4. After the miracle or answered prayer occurred, did you find there were other unresolved expectations around your situation you had not expected?

5. Do your friends and family support the transformations God brought to your life? Did they also hurt you in unexpected ways?

6. How did you cope with new fears that arose after the miracle occurred?

7. Have you ever experienced God giving you a new promise that you did not have ears to hear and could only recognize in hindsight?

8. What impacted you the most in this chapter?

VERSES TO CONTEMPLATE

2 Corinthians 12:9–10: But he (The Lord) said to me, "My grace is sufficient for you, for my power is made perfect in weakness."

Called to War Study Guide

13

Rest, Recuperation, and Reassignment

After getting injured in battle, soldiers are given time for rest and recuperation. This is what metaphorically happened in my life after the difficult pregnancy and birth of our first child. I may have been wounded, but God gave us a beautiful and amazing daughter who helped to heal our hearts after a decade of fighting. Our daughter also brought with her the gift of hope, which was a weapon we would need for the battles that remained in our future. In due time, hope gave us the courage to step back into the war on infertility even though several more painful losses remained on the horizon.

Our Commander was near, and he was always communicating, even if I didn't always understand the plans he was orchestrating in our lives. We maynot like the saying, "God works all things together for our good" but that doesn't make it any less true. Only the original life-giver can take the brokenness of our life and make something beautiful.

Here are a few questions to help you apply this chapter's material to your life:

1. Reflect on a part of your life story when difficulties and pain were swallowed up by hope

and joy. In what way does hope change your perspective on hardship?

2. What have you learned about the power of hope in this chapter?

3. Can you identify any place in your life where there is a juxtaposition between loss and hope? How do you handle this conflict?

4. Can you name all of the battles you face? Do you see any pattern or a way they might be connected to a larger story?

5. Do you recognize God's presence in your daily life? Do you see him working in your circumstances?

6. Can you identify with my comparison to a Magna Doodle? If so, in what way?

7. How do you currently feel about Romans 8:28? Can you embrace this truth yet?

8. What impacted you the most in this chapter?

VERSES TO CONTEMPLATE

Romans 8:28: And we know that in all things God works for the good of those who love him, who have been called according to his purpose.

Proverbs 13:12: Hope deferred makes the heart sick, but a longing fulfilled is a tree of life.

Chapter 13

14

The Final Battle

There comes a time for all wars to end. There are winners and losers, but nonetheless, surrender leads to peace, and peace eventually leads to new beginnings. In the stories of our lives, this looks like resolution to a conflict we've endured. As we explored a few chapters ago, this might occur upon surrendering to the plans that our Commander has for our lives. We may or may not get the baby, so to speak.

In this chapter, you learn how the Lord redeemed everything that was lost in my first birth experience. It's always so humbling to me that God cares about the details of our lives. He never stops writing our beautiful stories! You also read about my selah moment when the battle for my biological children finally came to an end fifteen years after it began. Infertility transformed me into a warrior, and yet I still didn't have the eyes to see all that the Lord planned for the transformation of my purpose or identity.

Here are a few questions to reflect as you consider the end of a war you've fought on your way to becoming someone new entirely:

1. What conditions would it take for you to continue battling for your promises?

Chapter 14

2. Have you been amazed by the adversity you face in some aspects of your life? How might this be tied to your destiny?

3. Have you experienced any double portion blessings in your life?

4. Do you continue to fight fear? If so, how do you deal with this obstacle?

5. Can you verbalize your heart's desire?

6. Can you see a place where God turned a situation around to redeem the details of your life like he did in the comparison of my two birth experiences?

7. Did you ever experience a "selah" moment?

8. What impacted you the most in this chapter?

VERSES TO CONTEMPLATE

Psalm 30:11–12: You turned my wailing into dancing; you removed my sackcloth and clothed me with joy, that my heart may sing your praises and not be silent. LORD my God, I will praise you forever.

Called to War Study Guide

15

A New War

After the war ends, the echo of battle continues to call to some and not to others. Some soldiers complete their initial military service and then transition out of the military to pursue a civilian life. Others. however, decide to make a career in the armed forces. There are many reasons to pursue either of these paths, but it seems a sense of duty, a calling to something bigger than oneself is often involved with those who continue to serve.

Metaphorically, I've stood at this great chasm between civilian and military life. But there was an echo, a sound that kept returning and repeating in my ears, that I could not ignore. Though our biological children had all arrived, our family was not complete. This forced me to examine the foundations of my life, the decisions I had made early in my infertility wars, and to choose to follow my Commander into another war. Amazing things happened as I leaned into where the Lord was leading in our story; he began to give me a new heart entirely and an ally who would fight alongside me in this next war.

Here are a few questions to help you relate this material to your story:

1. Understanding we are all called to war at some point in our spiritual lives, do you see yourself as a soldier who wants to transition out when your service is finished, or do you see yourself as career military?

Called to War Study Guide

2. As in my story, can you identify any subsequent "wars" that you voluntarily fought after your first war ended?

3. What echoes do you hear in your life? Have you responded to these sounds? If so, how?

4. Are there foundations in your life (family, legacy) that need repaired? How can you begin this work?

5. What might these foundations have to do with the echo?

6. Has God given you an ally in your war?

7. Do you recognize a place in your story where God fundamentally changed how you view a situation so much so that it altered the future course of your life?

8. What impacted you the most in this chapter?

VERSES TO CONTEMPLATE

Nehemiah 2:4–5: The king said to me, "What is it you want?" Then I prayed to the God of heaven, and I answered the king, "If it pleases the king and if your servant has found favor in his sight, let him send me to the city in Judah where my ancestors are buried so that I can rebuild it."

Isaiah 61:4: They will rebuild the ancient ruins and restore the places long devastated; they will renew the ruined cities that have been devastated for generations.

Chapter 15

16

Overseas Duty Station

Not everyone who is career military will receive orders for an overseas duty station. In keeping with the metaphorical comparisons here, it's also safe to say that not everyone who serves the Lord is called to some type of overseas missions work. However, I would venture to say that everyone experiences some type of change that is stretching and challenging, even if that change doesn't involve geography. Maybe your new orders were to move to a different church or to a different job. Or maybe your change required you to go back to school or remarry later in life. In any of these life-changing situations, changes and adjustments must be made and accepted to understand the new environment to which you've been called.

In our story, we were stepping into Guatemala and the world of international adoption at the same time. The learning curve was incredibly steep, and timing was a critical factor on many levels. This new war required new strategies, tactics, weapons, and alliances that were very different from my infertility war. No longer was my body the battleground for my babies either. We were caught between governments and global politics, not to mention unethical practices and flat-out lies that pushed us to our limits emotionally and financially.

Chapter 16

While adoption may not be the name of your war, here are a few questions to help you apply this chapter's material to your story:

1. Can you identify a change of duty station in your story?

2. In a particularly stretching season of your life, how did your heart cope? What new thing did you learn about yourself during this period?

3. Have you ever pursued something so big that it felt impossible toresolve/achieve? If so, how did you cope with the enormity of the situation?

4. Have you ever held something so precious in your arms only to be forced to let it go again? How did God help you through that process?

5. As I've done in this chapter with adoption, have you ever researched a Christian perspective on a situation/topic? What did you learn in that process?

6. What new strategies, tactics, or weapons did you need to acquire in your allegorical wars?

7. Have you ever been blatantly lied to or deceived? How did you resolve this conflict?

8. What impacted you the most in this chapter?

Verses to Contemplate

Ruth 1:16–18: But Ruth replied, "Don't urge me to leave you or to turn back from you. Where you go I will go, and where you stay I will stay. Your people will be my people and your God my God. Where you die I will die, and there I will be buried. May the LORD deal with me, be it ever so severely, if even death separates you and me." When Naomi realized that Ruth was determined to go with her, she stopped urging her.

17

Returning Home

In this chapter, we look at the idea of a two-front war and the difficulties of fighting separate battles at once. This scenario is more common than most of us would like, but nonetheless there are times in our lives where we are often stretched to our limit in opposing directions. We dream, sometimes for years, about what life will look like when the proverbial war is over and how peace will feel. Post-war life and subsequent homecomings are highly anticipated and greatly celebrated. Yet, reentry into normal life is also filled with unique challenges and emotional adjustments for those returning from war.

Our adoption wars raged in total for nearly three years. We were bringing home two children from Guatemala and both of the adoptions were fraught with difficulties and delays. I once again clung to worship to get me through all of the painful battles for our son and daughter. Eventually, our babies both came home to picture perfect homecomings and were well loved by many. While I was so thankful to finally be done battling for my family after twenty-three-years in war, I found myself stumbling through a post-adoption depression. My emotional state, combined with my baby girl's difficulty bonding, led me through one of the most challenging parts of my motherhood and some of the rawest material presented in this book.

Called to War Study Guide

Here are a few questions to help you relate this material to your story:

1. Can you recall any two-front wars you were called to fight?

2. One of my greatest weapons of war is worship. What is your greatest weapon?

3. Metaphorically, if you've already experienced the resolution of your war, how did the homecoming reality match up to your dreams?

4. What unexpected challenges did you face after your war(s) came to an end? What emotions did you experience?

5. Have you experienced trauma? If so, can you define your trauma?

6. My youngest daughter, and her rejection of me as a mother, taught me more about myself and the truth of parenting than any of my other children. Turning the mirror on yourself, what transformational truths have you learned about yourself in post-war life?

7. How has God helped make beauty from the ashes in your story?

8. What impacted you the most in this chapter?

Chapter 17

VERSES TO CONTEMPLATE

Acts 16:25–26: About midnight Paul and Silas were praying and singing hymns to God, and the other prisoners were listening to them. Suddenly there was such a violent earthquake that the foundations of the prison were shaken. At once all the prison doors flew open, and everyone's chains came loose.

Psalm 63:3–4: Because your love is better than life, my lips will glorify you. I will praise you as long as I live, and in your name I will lift up my hands.

18

Special Forces

During my last visit trip to Guatemala, I surrendered to a call to be a voice for the voiceless. Suddenly, I was able to see that through my entire story from being a twelve-year-old feeling a call to missions, through my twenty-three- years of infertility that brought me to Guatemala, God had been working in my life to create the heart of one called to serve. The calling did not look like anything I had thought when I was a child, but it was clear that my destiny in fighting all of my wars was not simply to build my own family. I had been called to war so that I would one day willingly fight for others.

Scripture makes it clear that our Commander enables us each with a unique call and specialized giftings (or talents). It is our responsibility to use these talents wisely in order that the purpose over our live may be fulfilled. For me, this meant going back to school to get qualified. For you, this might look like learning how to play the guitar or becoming a foster parent or caring for an aging parent. It turns out that God makes our hands to war so each of us can apply our unique fingerprint to a Kingdom purpose that is bigger than ourselves.

Here are a few questions to help you consider the unique way you are called to war:

Chapter 18

1. Has this book helped you understand that you are also called to war?

2. Do you know what you are called to war for?

3. What are the unique callings and giftings God has given to you?

4. Have you surrendered to a call? What was this experience in your life?

5. How can you get qualified or further develop your talents to support this calling?

6. Have you ever had to grow in the dark? If so, how did you feel during this season?

7. How have your wars prepared you for your destiny?

8. What impacted you the most in this chapter?

VERSES TO CONTEMPLATE

Psalm 144:1–2: Praise be to the LORD my Rock, who trains my hands for war, my fingers for battle. He is my loving God and my fortress, my stronghold and my deliverer, my shield, in whom I take refuge, who subdues peoples under me.

Romans 12:4–8: For just as each of us has one body with many members, and these members do not all have the same function, so in Christ we, though many, form one body, and each member belongs to all the others.

> We have different gifts, according to the grace given to each of us. If your gift is prophesying, then prophesy in accordance with your faith; if it is serving, then serve; if it is teaching, then teach; if it is to encourage, then give encouragement; if it is giving, then give generously; if it is to lead, do it diligently; if it is to show mercy, do it cheerfully.

19-20

New Eyes, New Heart, and a New Walk

Called to War is a book about faith and transformation. Although I share the stories of my infertility and adoption through figurative militaristic imagery, the point of this material is to help you embrace the battles God leads you through, and to reframe the difficulties you endure through a redemptive lens. Whatever path you are traversing, whatever has been denied or wherever you are in pain, I know confidently God has a purpose and even more importantly, that He is right there by your side. You are not alone. Trust him to lead you, guide you, and direct you as you discover the truth about your unique purpose and his exquisite plan for your life.

As we complete this study guide, I want to encourage you to pick up those heavenly weapons of war you need to fight your battles. Trust your Commander, who is the author and finisher of your faith, to transform your life and give you new eyes, a new heart, and a new walk. You can do hard things! God is for you! Expect the victory! Embrace your repurposed life!

A few closing questions to consider:

Called to War Study Guide

1. Can you see the places where God is transforming your life?

2. Have you ever endured a confusing uprooting season?

3. Where have you leaned into an unknown future before you could clearly see what was happening? How did this make you feel?

4. Have you explored a promised land? Were you fearful or full of faith?

5. What giants stand ahead of your new day?

6. Are you willing to follow the Lord … immediately?

7. In what ways has the material in Called to War brought you hope?

8. What impacted you the most in this chapter?

Verses to Contemplate

Joshua 1:9: Have I not commanded you? Be strong and courageous. Do not be afraid; do not be discouraged, for the LORD your God will be with you wherever you go."

Matthew 4:18–22: As Jesus was walking beside the Sea of Galilee, he saw two brothers, Simon called Peter and his brother Andrew. They were casting a net into the lake, for they were fishermen. "Come, follow me," Jesus said, "and I will send you out to fish for people."

Chapter 19–20

At once they left their nets and followed him. Going on from there, he saw two other brothers, James son of Zebedee and his brother John. They were in a boat with their father Zebedee, preparing their nets. Jesus called them, and immediately they left the boat and their father and followed him.

ABOUT THE AUTHOR

Dawn Amsden Stark is a change agent, a storyteller, a promise seeker, and a beach lover. Professionally, she is a development manager for Operation Blessing, where she matches the philanthropic goals and interests of partners to the needs of the most vulnerable worldwide. Purposely, she is the founder of {Re}Purposed Lives, a social business that supports at-risk children and families while reducing textile waste, through recycling unwanted stuffed animals and plush toys.

Dawn holds a BA in government and international relations from Regent University and an MA in international community development from Southeastern University.

She lives in Sarasota, Florida, with her husband of thirty-six years, five children, and their Siberian Husky puppy. *Called to War* is her debut release.

In dedication of Dawn's calling to be a voice for the voiceless, 20 percent of the proceeds from *Called to War* will be donated to reputable organizations serving at-risk children and families—both here in the US and around the world. For more details on the organizations benefitting from sales of this book, please visit RepurposedLives.com.

Follow Dawn

DAWNAMSDENSTARK.COM

 AuthorDawnAmsdenStark

 DawnAmsdenStark

www.ingramcontent.com/pod-product-compliance
Lightning Source LLC
Chambersburg PA
CBHW072209100526
44589CB00015B/2441